Super Senses

Tasting

Mary Mackill

Raintree

www.raintreepublishers.co.uk

Visit our website to find out more information about **Raintree** books.

To order:
☎ Phone 44 (0) 1865 888112
▤ Send a fax to 44 (0) 1865 314091
▢ Visit the Raintree Bookshop at **www.raintreepublishers.co.uk** to browse our catalogue and order online.

First published in Great Britain by Raintree,
Halley Court, Jordan Hill, Oxford OX2 8EJ,
part of Harcourt Education.
Raintree is a registered trademark of Harcourt
Education Ltd.

Editorial: Kate Bellamy
Design: Jo Hinton-Malivoire and bigtop
Illustrations: Darren Lingard
Picture Research: Hannah Taylor and Fiona Orbell
Production: Helen McCreath

Originated by Chroma Graphics (Overseas) Pte. Ltd
Printed and bound in China by
South China Printing Company

ISBN 1 406 20022 0 (hardback)
ISBN 978 1 406 20022 5 (hardback)
10 09 08 07 06
10 9 8 7 6 5 4 3 2 1
ISBN 1 406 20029 8 (paperback)
ISBN 978 1 406 20029 4 (paperback)
11 10 09 08 07
10 9 8 7 6 5 4 3 2 1

British Library Cataloguing in Publication Data
Mackill, Mary
Tasting – (Super Senses)
612.8'7
A full catalogue record for this book is available
from the British Library.

Acknowledgements
The publishers would like to thank the following
for permission to reproduce photographs:
Alamy Images pp. **9** (Image Source Spirit), **6**, **14**,
23c (MedioImages Fresca Collection); Bubbles
p. **4** (Loisjoy Thurstun); Corbis pp. **13**, **21b**, **21d**
(royalty free), **17** (Hurewitz Creative), **18** (Steve
Kaufman); Getty Images pp. **11** (Digital Vision),
10 (FoodPix), **15** (Image Source), **16** (PhotoAlto),
5, **21a**, **21c**, **23b** (Photodisc), **7**, **23a** (Stone), **12**
(Taxi); Harcourt Education Ltd pp. **22** (Gareth
Boden), **20** (Tudor Photography);
Photolibrary.com p. **19**.

Cover photograph reproduced with permission of
Warling Studios.

Every effort has been made to contact copyright
holders of any material reproduced in this book.
Any omissions will be rectified in subsequent
printings if notice is given to the publishers.

The paper used to print this book comes from
sustainable resources.

Contents

Some words are shown in bold, **like this**. They are explained in the glossary on page 23.

What are my senses?

You have five **senses**. They help you to see, hear, taste, smell, and touch things.

Pretend you are at a party.

What can you taste?

Tasting is one of your five senses.

What do I use to taste?

tongue

You taste with your **tongue**.

There are **taste buds** on your tongue.

Your taste buds **sense** the **flavours** of food.

How does my sense of taste work?

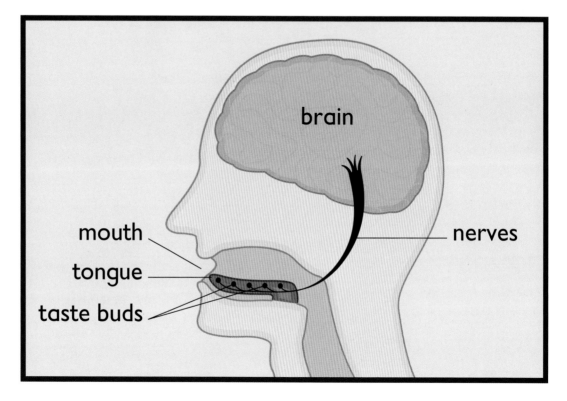

brain

mouth

tongue

taste buds

nerves

Your **taste buds** have **nerves** in them.

The nerves send a message to your brain.

Your brain picks up the message.

Your brain would tell you that the lemon is sour!

What can I taste?

salty

sweet

You can taste different **flavours**.

You can taste food that is sweet or salty.

bitter

sour

You can taste bitter
and sour foods too.

How does tasting help me?

Food that is bad for you can taste bitter.

The taste stops you wanting to eat it!

You can taste food from all over
the world!

How can I taste things better?

Your **sense** of taste and smell work together.

Smelling food helps you to taste it better.

Try to stay healthy.

It is harder to smell and taste food when you have a cold.

How can I look after my sense of taste?

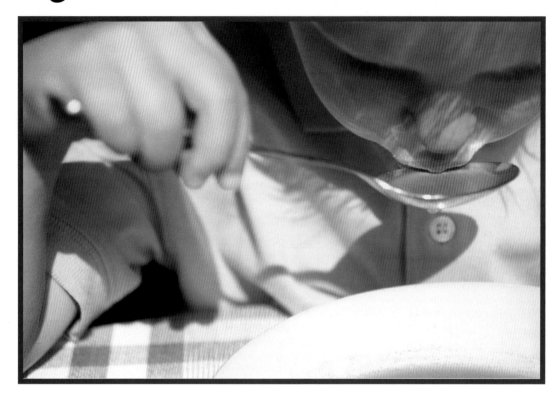

Look after your **tongue**.

Food that is too hot will hurt your tongue.

Eat different foods.

Your **taste buds** will learn how other **flavours** taste.

Animals can taste too!

Animals use their **sense** of taste to eat good food.

Some birds love to taste sweet things.

Did you know a catfish has **taste buds** all over its body?

Test your sense of taste

Ask a friend to taste some food.

Is it sweet, salty, bitter, or sour?

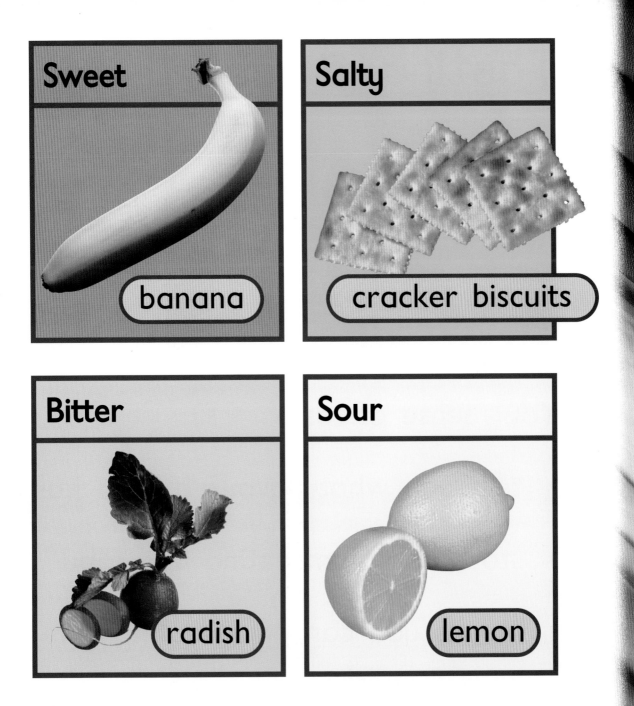

Sweet

banana

Salty

cracker biscuits

Bitter

radish

Sour

lemon

Can you think of other sweet, salty, bitter, and sour foods?

Tasting is super!

Your **sense** of taste:

- tells you what **flavour** a food has

- stops you from eating bad food

- means you can enjoy eating with your friends!

Glossary

 **flavour** taste of a food. The four main flavours are sweet, salty, sour, and bitter.

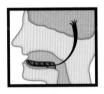 **nerves** parts inside your body. Nerves work with the brain to sense things.

 **sense** something that helps you to see, touch, taste, smell, and hear the things around you

 **taste buds** special parts on your tongue that sense the flavour of food

 **tongue** part in your mouth used to taste food

Index

Note to Parents and Teachers

Reading for information is an important part of a child's literacy development. Learning begins with a question about something. Help children think of themselves as investigators and researchers by encouraging their questions about the world around them. Each chapter in this book begins with a question. Read the question together. Look at the pictures. Talk about what you think the answer might be. Then read the text to find out if your predictions were correct. Think of other questions you could ask about the topic, and discuss where you might find the answers. Assist children in using the picture glossary and the index to practice new vocabulary and research skills.